William Henry Arnoux

The Dutch in America

Vol. 1

William Henry Arnoux

The Dutch in America
Vol. 1

ISBN/EAN: 9783337309527

Printed in Europe, USA, Canada, Australia, Japan

Cover: Foto ©ninafisch / pixelio.de

More available books at **www.hansebooks.com**

THE DUTCH IN AMERICA.

A HISTORICAL ARGUMENT

BY

WILLIAM HENRY ARNOUX.

NEW YORK.
PRIVATELY PRINTED.
1890.

PREFACE.

The following pages were presented to the Court of Appeals in the State of New York as an argument in an elevated railroad case then pending, in which the fundamental question involved was whether the Dutch Roman law prevailed in Manhattan Island before 1664, under which law the railroad claimed that the State absolutely owned the streets and that adjacent owners had no rights or easements therein. This question depended upon the determination of the historical question who, under the law of nations, discovered and settled New York. To aid the Court in the solution of this problem this argument was written.

THE DUTCH IN AMERICA.

In 1632, when the ambassador of the Netherlands at the Court of St. James, entered into diplomatic correspondence with the government to which he was accredited, on behalf of the Dutch West India Company, to obtain the release of a Dutch vessel which was detained in an English port, "it provoked," says Mrs. Lamb, in her History of New York, "another spirited correspondence between the two nations. The Dutch statesmen claimed that they had discovered the Hudson River in 1609, that some of their people had returned there in 1610; that a specific trading charter had been granted in 1614; that a fort and garrison had been maintained there until the formation, in 1623, of the West India Company, which has since occupied the country; and great stress was laid upon the purchase of the land from its aboriginal owners." Subsequently other claims were made that events showed the exercise and recognition of sovereignty between 1611 and 1653, and of a title under the grant made of the New World to Spain by Pope Alexander VII. These we shall consider in the following order :

1. Title by purchase from the Indians.

2. Title by the discovery of Hudson.

3. Title under the Borgian grant to Spain.

4. Title acquired after 1611 (exclusive of the Indian purchase).

6

It was never contended that either by original recognition or by subsequent acquiescence, the English had estopped themselves from asserting whatever rights they may have at any time acquired, and after examining the claims above set forth it will be shown herein that such contention would have been without the slightest justification.

1. *Title by purchase from the Indians.*

In 1626, it has been asserted, the Governor of the Dutch West India Company bought the Island of Manhattan, then supposed to contain 24,000 acres of land, for the paltry sum of twenty-four dollars. If a document preserved in the collection of the Pennsylvania Historical Society is genuine, this was a fraudulent transaction. The unscrupulous Dutchman negotiated with the tribe of the Manhatoes, who occupied the island, and whose wigwams were located on the shore of the little lake afterwards called the Collect, which was situated between Broadway and the Bowery, having its outlet eastwardly into the East River, for a piece of land for his back garden. When the bargain was consummated he claimed the whole island beyond his house. Without discussing the morality of the matter we shall accept the Dutch version as presented in the address of the Assembly of XIX. to the States-General, in Oct., 1634, which was as follows : "After the county had passed into the hands of the incorporated West India Company, said company purchased from the Indians, who were the indubitable owners thereof, the Island of Manhattan, situate at the entrance of said river, and there laid the foundation of a city," and examine only the legal effect.

"America, separated from Europe by a wide ocean," says Ch.-J. Marshall, in the case of Worcester *vs.* State of Georgia, 6 Peters, 574, "was inhabited by a distinct people, divided into separate nations, independent of each other, and of the rest of the world, having institutions of their own and governing themselves by their own laws. It is difficult to comprehend the proposition that the inhabitants of either quarter of the globe could have rightful original claims of dominion over the inhabitants of the other, or over the land they occupied, or that the discovery of either by the other should give the discoverer right in the country he discovered, which annulled the pre-existing rights of its ancient possessors."

In Johnson *vs.* McIntosh, 8 Wheat., 543, 591, the same great jurist said : "However extravagant the pretension of converting the discovery of an inhabited country into conquest may appear; if the principle has been asserted in the first instance, and afterwards sustained; if a country has been acquired and held under it; if the property of the great mass of the community originates in it, it becomes the law of the land, and cannot be questioned. So, too, with respect to the concomitant principle that the Indian inhabitants are to be considered merely as occupants to be protected indeed, while in peace, in the possession of their land, but to be deemed incapable of transferring the title to others : however this restriction may be opposed to natural right, and to the usage of civilized nations, yet if it be indispensable to that system under which the country has been settled, and be adapted to the actual condition of the two people, it may perhaps be supported by reason, and certainly cannot be rejected by courts of justice."

"So far as respected the rights of the crown no distinction was taken between vacant land and land occupied by the Indians. The title, subject only to the right of occupancy of the Indians, was admitted to be in the king."

Subsequently the same question was discussed by Ch.-J. Taney in Martin *vs.* Waddell, 16 Pet., 367, and it was there decided that the Indians were simply tenants, having only a usufructuary interest in the soil, without any title thereto ; but, as Marshall said, only the rightful sovereign could acquire such right.

As it is said in Wadsworth *vs.* Buffalo Hydraulic Association, 15 Barb., 89: "It is true that the Indian title has been styled simply a right of occupancy, and the European sovereigns discovering the country claimed the ultimate title. The course, however, adopted was to acquire the title of the Indians by treaty, and the right to make treaties appertained to the sovereignty."

This whole question has been disposed of in a single sentence of Brown, J., in the Town of Southampton *vs.* The Mecox Bay Oyster Co., 116 N. Y., 7: "Nor did the Indians have any title to the land which they could grant, and which could be recognized in the courts of this country."

This is not a new principle of law announced in this country, or in this century. It was the settled doctrine of Europe in the sixteenth century, and it could not be successfully controverted by the jurists of Holland. They were therefore compelled to supplement it by the assertion that they were the original discoverers of the region, and therefore the Indian title ratified that which they had previously acquired.

Unless it can be established that the Dutch were the discoverers it inevitably follows that their Indian title was a nullity.

2. *Title by the discovery of Hudson.*

It is an incontrovertible fact that our first accurate and definite knowledge of the existence of the noble river that bears the name of Hudson is due to that intrepid navigator. There was a corporation in England named the Muscovy Company, in whose service Henry Hudson had made several voyages in the northern seas, in which he had made such a reputation that the East India Company employed him to discover a route to India by way of Greenland. Of course the attempt was a failure. He was engaged by said company to make a second voyage, in which, adopting the suggestion of Capt. John Smith, he sailed to Maine, and on the 4th day of September, 1609, reached the Hudson River, which he hoped would prove an arm of the South Sea, and by which he could accomplish his desired end. He ascended the river as far as Albany, where he discovered that the river which he supposed would lead him to India was becoming an unnavigable stream. He therefore abandoned the attempt, returned to England, and never visited the place again.

This, however, alone does not establish that he was the discoverer, either actually or in a legal sense. The English have never disputed that Hudson made this voyage. On the contrary, they were proud of it, and they, not the Dutch, gave his name to the river. They base their claim upon priority. Each government acknowledges the same principle of law.

"We derive our rights in America," said Edmund Burke, "from the discovery of Sebastian Cabot, who first made the North American continent in 1497. The fact is sufficiently certain to establish a right to our settlements in America." "To this discovery," says Marshall, in Johnson *vs.* McIntosh. 8 Wheat., 576, "the English trace their title." The same view is presented by Taney: "The English possession in America was not claimed by right of conquest, but by right of discovery."

Every historian, every geographer, every jurist and every English statesman concur on this point. What is the fact?

The discovery of Columbus aroused the curiosity and the cupidity of all Europe. The news of a new world stimulated every adventurer in every other maritime country to find a new course to the Indies. A

refugee from Venice, whose anglicized name was
John Cabot, who resided in Bristol, then the chief
port of England, petitioned Henry VII., King of
England, to authorize him to embark on a voyage
of discovery. The King made the grant with that
frugal mind that made him the richest sovereign in
Europe, on condition that he should receive one-
seventh of the profits of the voyage. The merchants
of Bristol provided him with a fleet and its equip-
ments, and, with his three sons, he set sail for Ice-
land; thence changing his course to the westward, he
eventually reached land which he supposed, to the
day of his death, was the eastern coast of Asia, in the
territory of the Grand Cham. It was on St. John's
Day, the 10th day of June, 1497, that he landed.
It was on the coast of Labrador, and is supposed to
have been Cape Breton. The exact spot can never
be absolutely determined. It is certain that he first
in modern times discovered and landed upon the
continent of America. Following the custom of the
times, when he landed he planted first the cross, then
the English standard, and finally the banner of St.
Mark's, the ensign of his beloved Venice. He then
formally took possession of the territory in the
name of the King of England, and named it St.
John's in honor of the day.

The legal effect of this transaction has been adjudicated by the Supreme Court of the United States,
in the opinion of Marshall, in the case against the
State of Georgia before cited.

"This principle, suggested by the actual state of
things, was that discovery gave title to the government by whose subjects or by whose authority it
was made against all other European governments,
which title might be consummated by possession.
This principle, acknowledged by all Europeans,
because it was the interest of all to acknowledge it,
gave to the nation making the discovery, as its
inevitable consequence, the sole right of acquiring
the soil, and of making settlements on it. It was

an exclusive principle, which shut out the right of competition among those who had agreed to it. * * It regulates the right given by discovery among the European discoverers."

In the McIntosh case, he also treats the same subject: " It is supposed to be a principle of universal law that if an uninhabited country be discovered by a number of individuals who acknowledge no connection with and owe no allegiance to any government whatever, the country becomes the property of the discoverer, so far at least as they can use it. They acquire a title in common. The title of the whole land is the whole society. It is to be divided and parcelled out according to the will of the society, expressed by the whole body, or by that organ which is authorized by the whole to express it. If the discovery be made, and possession of the country be taken, under the authority of existing government which is acknowledged by the immigrants, it is supposed to be equally well settled that the discovery is made for the whole nation, that the country becomes a part of the nation, and that the vacant soil is to be disposed of by that organ of the government which has the constitutional power to dispose of the national domains, by that organ in which all vacant territory is vested by law.

" According to the theory of the British Constitution, all vacant lands are vested in the crown, as representing the nation, and the exclusive power to grant them is admitted to reside in the crown, as a branch of the royal prerogative."

Under this determination of the law the act of Cabot in taking possession of the continent where he landed vested its title in the British crown.

After performing this momentous deed, by which England became the owner of a territory of almost illimitable extent, Cabot sailed along the coast southward, as far as the 38° north latitude, that is, to the Capes of the Delaware; then returned to England and reported his success.

The following year, 1498, Cabot presented a second petition to the King and obtained a renewal of his concessions, upon which he, with his son Sebastian, crossed the Atlantic and skirted the shore of America from Labrador to the Gulf of Mexico. The father died before his return, leaving the expedition to the care of Sebastian. "Did these adventurers, by sailing along the coast, and occasionally landing on it, acquire for the several governments to which they belonged, or by whom they were commissioned, a rightful property to the soil from the Atlantic to the Pacific, or rightful dominion over the numerous people who occupied it?" It seems absurd to claim that such voyages could give England ownership to the land upon which the mariners had scarcely gazed. This question, propounded by Marshall, he indirectly, but conclusively, answered thus : "But power, war, conquest, give rights which, after possession, are conceded by the world and which can never be controverted by those on whom they descend."

Under the law of nations these two voyages of the Cabots gave to England the exclusive title to three thousand miles in latitude of the American continent, as the original discoverer, besides the untold riches of the deep in the food fisheries of Newfoundland and the whale fisheries of the Arctic sea, in which she shared with other nations.

Sebastian Cabot, whose name has eclipsed his father's, inherited the patent given to his father, which entitled him to the exclusive possession and occupation of all the lands which he had thus discovered. To us the stupendous folly of that age is utterly incomprehensible. This vast continent, with a wealth not yet developed, but exceeding the most daring flight of the miser's avarice, invited England to take possession, and the invitation was rejected for nearly a century. Cabot endeavored fruitlessly for years to enlist the capital of Englishmen to prosecute his discoveries, and in 1512 left

England disheartened at his disappointment, and engaged in the service of the King of Spain. Subsequently, in 1548, he returned to England. In March, 1551, he was granted a pension by the King, which was renewed by Queen Anne in November, 1555. On the 27th day of May, 1557, he resigned this pension, and in or about 1559 he died unhonored and unknown. The date of his death, the place of his burial, are forgotten. No stone marks his last resting place. No monument in England, which he so greatly enriched, or in America, which owes him such a debt of gratitude, commemorates the fame of the original discoverer of America. The irony of fate has ordained that the name of Columbus should shed lustre upon the reign of Ferdinand and Isabella, although he brought to the Spanish crown a gift that proved its destruction, while Cabot, who by this discovery laid the foundation of England's greatness, wealth and power, is forgotten.

The grant to Cabot expired with his death, and for nearly twenty years thereafter not a man in England thought it worth his while to even ask for a similar privilege. There was, however, one individual, Sir Humphrey Gilbert, who had a scientific interest in exploring, who conceived an idea, such as now exists, in the endeavor to reach the North pole. He firmly believed that there existed a northern passage to Asia, and that, if stations were founded from which explorations could be conducted, that passage would be discovered. On the 11th day of June, 1578, Elizabeth, then Queen of England, granted to Sir Humphrey a patent of all lands in America two hundred leagues in either direction north and south from the place of his landing, and from ocean to ocean. So worthless was this Continent! Sir Humphrey had a half brother, twenty-six years of age, named Walter Ralegh, who already had achieved a heroic career, first fighting as a volunteer in aid of the Huguenots in France, and afterwards assisting the Dutch

in their patriotic struggle against Spain, and
to whom he intrusted the command of one
of the fleet of seven vessels with which
he sailed from England in November, 1578, with
three hundred and fifty men. Unfortunately the
season was unpropitious, and the voyagers were
compelled to return without having accomplished
anything. Nothing daunted, the noble knight in
June, 1583, again sailed for America with a fleet of
four vessels and the good wishes of Elizabeth, but
without his half brother, who had become one of the
Queen's favorites, and she forbade his thus risking
his life.

He arrived at St. John, on the shores of Newfoundland, in August, and, as he writes, "On the
fifth of August I entered here in the right of the
Crown of England, and have engraved the arms of
England, divers Spaniards, Portuguese and other
strangers witnessing the same." Then he sailed for
Norumbega, and in latitude 40° lost his great ship,
the "Admiral," with most of his supplies. This
disaster compelled him to set sail for England, and
on the way thither his little craft foundered in mid-
ocean, and he and all his crew perished.

On the 20th day of March, 1584, Walter Ralegh
obtained from Elizabeth a similar grant of all land
extending two hundred leagues north and south of
any point where he might locate a colony. His
patent authorized Ralegh to detain and possess, as
lawful prize, all citizens of England and all other
persons in amity with us, their ships, goods and
furniture, who should trade to the new found lands
without Ralegh's consent. And that he might
expel and resist any who should inhabit in the
lands granted without his assent. Giving unto him
full power and authority to take and surprise by
all manner of means whatsoever all and every person, their ships, goods and furniture, which, without his license, shall be found trafficing in any
harbors or creeks within said territory.

On the 4th day of July, 1584, the first English speaking colony landed in the territory of the United States. Thus the foundation of the nation, and the establishment of the nation's liberties, have the same anniversary. This landing was made at the haven of New Inlet, where they "took possession in the name of the Queen's most excellent Majesty, as rightful Queen and Princess of the same." The settlement was subsequently made on Roanoke Island, but it was of short duration, for in June, 1586, the colonists returned to England. In 1589 Ralegh granted a patent to "the Governor and assistants of the City of Raleigh in Virginia," as he had named the country in honor of the virgin queen, who had in turn conferred upon him the rank of Knight. Before the end of the century Ralegh had sent out eight colonies and had expended £40,000, an immense sum in those days. He had an abiding faith in the future of America. "I shall live to see an empire on its shores," was his prophetic utterance, the fulfilment of which was prevented by his untimely death.

In 1602, a Capt. Gosnold sailed from England with some colonists, whom he landed on the Island of Cuttyhunk, and returned with a cargo of sassafras and cedar wood. Upon his arrival in England, Sir Walter Raleigh had his cargo confiscated in the Court of Queen's Bench, under the clauses of his charter from Elizabeth above cited, because he trespassed upon his domain without license from him. Thus, so far as the English Courts could determine, Ralegh had a valid title to the territory from New Inlet to Massachusetts, and it follows that that title included the whole of New York at the seaboard.

The following year England's greatest queen was succeeded by the son of her hated rival, and Ralegh's fortunes suffered a great eclipse. In November, 1603, this unworthy monarch, James I., caused the arrest, attainder and conviction of Ralegh for treason. Under the law of England the execution of the sentences is not essential for the forfeiture or escheat of the convict's property. Petersdorff, in his Abridgment, says, "By the verdict of guilty, goods and chattels are forfeited to the Crown; upon judgment in attainder the laws are divested." Blackstone states the law thus, "By attainder in high treason a man forfeited to the Crown all his lands and tenements of inheritance." Consequently, under the forms of law, this immense territory, which Elizabeth had granted to Ralegh, reverted to the Crown in 1603.

On the 16th day of April, 1606, King James made the famous charter to the Virginia colony. By it the patentees are divided into two classes, which are severally designated as the First Colony of Virginia and the Second Colony of Virginia. The territory assigned to the first colony extended from 34° to 41°; to the second colony from 39° to 45°. It will be observed that the land from 34° to 39° and from 41° to 45° was to be enjoyed severally by the respective colonies, and that from 39° to 41°, which embraces New York and the adjacent territory, was patented to both as tenants in common. It was intended as a neutral zone, over which both might enjoy a common jurisdiction.

This charter, which is too long to be reproduced here, contains, among other provisions, one by which the patentees were empowered "for their several defenses, to encounter, expulse, repel and resist all persons who shall, without license," attempt to inhabit "within the said precincts and limits of the said several colonies, or that shall interfere or attempt, at any time hereafter, the least detriment or annoyance of the said several colonies or plantations."

The nature of grants of this character has been examined and determined by the Supreme Court of the United States. It was a royal grant, revocable by the sovereign, so far as the lands remained in possession of the original patentees. As there is no waste or

unoccupied land of the Crown, so there is no waste
or unoccupied land of the viceroy. All made the
same claim. " France claimed all Canada and Acadia
at a time when the French population was very in-
considerable, and the Indians occupied almost the
whole country. No one of the powers of Europe
gave its assent to this principle more unequivocally
than England."

The right of England to this territory, stretching
from the boundary of North Carolina to the northern part of Maine, under the name of Virginia, was
officially recognized by the Dutch Government. On
the 24th day of April, 1608, the year before Hudson
sailed on the voyage to New York, on a petition presented to the States-General of Holland, requesting
it, leave of absence to Sir Thomas Gates, a Captain
of English soldiers in their employ, was granted for
one year, " to command in the country of Virginia
in colonizing the said countries."

Thus England discovered, named, patented and
colonized the territory in question before a single
Dutchman had ever visited the coast of America.

No one can read the records, which have thus
been briefly mentioned, without being convinced
that the Dutch had no claim of title to New York
by discovery under the voyage of Hudson.

It will, however, be wise to recur to the explorations of other nations, which will establish, not only
that the Dutch never had any claim to the discovery
of America, but in fact, they were the very last to
explore these shores.

The Portuguese, who had been the first maritime
nation of Europe, and who had discovered the way
to the Indies by doubling the Cape of Good Hope,
sought to find a more direct course to the Orient.
In the Summer of 1500 Gasper Cortereal, having
obtained from Emanuel, then King of Portugal, a
license to discover new islands, sailed from Lisbon
to the northward, and returned with a report that
he had landed in a beautiful country which he named

Terre Verde. The next year he renewed his search, and sailed along the coast of North America for six hundred leagues, without finding any end to the land, and therefore concluded that there was no passage to the Indies to be found there. In 1502 his brother Miguel sailed to North America, and made a closer exploration, in which he found many estuaries, large rivers and safe havens.

In 1524 Giovanni de Verrazano, a Florentine, under the authority of Francis I., King of France, sailed to North America with the intention of reaching Cathay, on the extreme coast of Asia. He explored from the Tropic of Capricorn to the 50° north latitude. On the way he visited a bay with a "grandissima riviere," and from thence sailed one hundred and fifty miles eastward to a bay with several islands, in the latitude of Rome, which has been identified with Newport. Consequently, the bay and river he had previously seen could have been only the bay of New York and the Hudson River. Doubts have been expressed regarding the veracity of this discovery, which have been argued with such force that Mr. Bancroft, in the later edition of his History of the United States, has omitted all reference to Verrazano which the previous edition contained. No serious question has been made that the author of the description had visited New York and Newport. It was contended that it was a forgery in attributing it to Verrazano. No commission to him can be found in the French archives, and the letter purporting to have been written by Verrazano to the King was of later origin. Recent discoveries have established, beyond all reasonable doubt, the authenticity of this letter, and the priority of Verrazano's discovery of the Hudson River.

In February, 1525, Esteban Gomez, a Portuguese, who had been the chief pilot of Magellan, under a concession from the King of Spain for an expedition to the northwest, to find a passage to Asia, sailed from Corunna, a port in the north of Spain, and

was absent for ten months. He coasted from Florida
to 41° north latitude, and on the 13th of June he
likewise discovered a large river in latitude 40° to
41°, which he named Rio de Antonio, in honor of St.
Anthony, whose day it was. Not content with visit-
ing the harbor, he sailed up the river, and in honor
of his discovery the Spanish seamen who followed
in his track, and were familiar with the river, called
it Rio de Gamas.

These adventurers returned with information of
the teeming food fishes which have always abounded
on the coast off the Banks. And all the seamen of
Western Europe, particularly the hardy fishermen
of Gascony, Spain and Portugal, frequented these
waters for cargoes of fish. For nearly a century the
customary route to America was to sail to the Azores,
then to the West Indies, and thence along the coast
of America to the fishing grounds, and to return by
retracing their course. It was in the presence of
these fishermen Sir Humphrey Gilbert took possession of the main land, and it was in following
their route, near the Azores, that his "little frigate"
foundered.

In coasting along the shore these fishermen had
several ports of refuge from storms, which they
called stages, one of which was this Rio de Gamas,
now known as the Hudson. In a map presented by
certain Dutch captains to the States General in 1611,
which has been preserved to this day, and which
represents the Hudson and the adjacent country as
far north as Albany, there are names of undoubted
Spanish origin. And "the Pompey stone," preserved in the State collection at Albany, the genu-
ineness of which is undoubted, and which is now
supposed to record the death of a Spanish captive
in or near the town of Pompey, also proves that the
Spaniards had made their way to the headwaters
of the river before the advent of the Dutch.

In 1534 Jacques Cartier, under a commission from
the King of France, founded a settlement in Canada;

and in 1564 Ribault and Landonniere, under a commission from Charles IX., colonized the Carolinas, and the French claimed all the intermediate territory. The name Norumbega, which they gave the country, has been derived from the corruption of the original name they gave to the Palisades, that high basaltic formation on the western bank of the river, *l'enorme berge* (the enormous cliffs). The English always conceded that the French had territorial rights. They only disputed their extent.

English, French, Portuguese and Spanish had visited the region. The French had originally discovered the harbor and river, the Spanish had explored it. The fishermen of all had made it a place of refuge. Then came the Dutch. In 1596 certain Dutch merchants obtained from the States-General of Holland the incorporation of a company known as "The Greenland Company" which proposed by that northerly route to find a way to the Indies. In 1598 some of their ships, avoiding the rigor of the Arctic Winter, entered the port of New York—perhaps having knowledge of it as one of the stages of the fishermen—and their crews built some temporary huts on Manhattan Island, where they wintered. In the Spring they departed, and no native of Holland ever returned until the famous voyage of Henry Hudson, eleven years afterwards.

The claim of the Dutch to title by discovery, under the voyage of Hudson, must, under the foregoing facts, be considered exploded. When in 1654 the States-General directed the West India Company to present their pretensions to the British Government, they were limited to reckoning from the beginning of 1611 and to conclude with 1650. When they proceeded to do this, and sent a delegation with it to England, they wrote back to Holland that they themselves did not consider the claim of the Company substantiated by the evidence adduced, and unless better evidence was brought forward they could not possibly press the claim upon the English Government (3 Asher, 35). Equally indefensible must the claim as discoverers be considered.

3. *Title under the Borgian grant.*

This claim seems to have been a *dernier* resort, and not to have been very seriously pressed. Its examination carries us back to a period anterior to the discovery of America.

When commerce was piracy, and might was right, the Church was the acknowledged superior and ultimate arbiter of the civilized world. Under the promise in the Messianic psalm,

" Ask of me
And I will give thee the heathen for thine inheritance
And the uttermost parts of the earth for thy possession,"

the Pope was conceded to have the right to dispose of all the territory inhabited by savages.

When the Turks captured Constantinople, and Venice entered into a treaty with the Sultan of Egypt, which gave it a monopoly of the commerce to the East, the wealth of which Europe had lately learned, through the travels of Marco Paulo and other adventurers into Asia, the endeavor of Europe was to find a new way to the Indies. Arabian knowledge, especially in navigation and astronomy, was slowly diffused through the Mediterranean, until the belief became general that the earth was not the flat plane patristic geography had taught but a globe, and that Africa was a mighty peninsula.

These ideas, developed by the Portuguese, who were aided by the newly discovered mariner's compass by which they could venture boldly on the shoreless main, led to the discovery of the coast of Guinea, the Cape of Good Hope, and, finally, to the coveted goal of the Indies.

Dutiful sons of the Church as they were, they did not claim to own this territory by right of discovery, but they applied to the Pope for a grant of the whole of the maritime East. This petition received a favorable answer, and they thereby obtained a monopoly of the whole of the East, from Cape Non to India.

But Venice and Portugal were not destined to have this rich traffic wholly undisturbed. An enthusiast and speculative dreamer of Genoa, named Columbus, went from Court to Court, endeavoring to obtain a fleet to sail westward to India, for he reasoned that, if the world were truly a sphere, the East could be found in the West, and he had observed, in his voyages among the islands in the Atlantic near Europe, that the westerly gales had wafted to their shores unknown vegetation, which must have come from land to the westward. For many long and weary years the Bible and common sense defeated his project. The theologians said, how could it be said that every eye should behold the Lord at His second coming, if there were people on the other side of the globe, and the wise, practical men wanted to know how the ships could sail up hill back again. At last Spanish cupidity overcame such unanswerable logic, and Columbus became immortal.

In the Spring of 1493, after the return of the discoverer of the New World, Ferdinand and Isabella, faithful to the traditions of the Church that the Pope, as Viceregent of God, had the absolute power of disposing of all land occupied by the heathen, sent a deputation to Rome, to Pope Alexander VII., petitioning for a grant of the newly discovered lands. The Pope, mindful of the previous donation to Portugal, made a grant by which he gave to Spain all continents and islands, known and unknown, discovered and to be discovered, lying west of a meridional line, to be drawn from pole to pole, one hundred miles west of the Azores, and confirmed to Portugal all to the eastward of such line.

How did this grant affect Holland ?

Mary, of Burgundy, brought to her husband, Maximilian, of Austria, as her dowry, the provinces of the Netherlands. Her son married Joanna, the daughter of Ferdinand and Isabella, the issue of which union was Charles V., Emperor of Austria, King of Spain, Duke of the Netherlands, and ruler over one-third of the habitable globe, the most powerful sovereign the world had seen since the destruction of the Roman empire.

That wonderful war between Holland and Spain, which lasted eighty years, and ended with Holland independent and prosperous, and with Spain crippled and impoverished, was primarily undertaken by Charles to enforce the obedience of his disloyal and rebellious subjects. The glowing pages of Motley worthily record the heroic struggle, in which, on the 26th day of July, 1581, the United Provinces, assembled at the Hague, solemnly declared their independence of the King of Spain and renounced their allegiance forever.

The pretensions of the Dutch to an interest in this Borgian grant were simply absurd. It was made before they were part of the Spanish Empire, and asserted by them after they had achieved their independence. Besides, Spain herself never claimed that the Papal grant conferred upon her any title to any part of America, north of Florida. "Spain," says Marshall in Johnson vs. McIntyre, "did not rest her title solely on the grant of the Pope. Her discussions respecting boundary with France, with Great Britain, and the United States all show that she placed it on the rights given by discovery." And the Dutch could obtain no larger right under this donation than the Spanish had for themselves.

In addition to these considerations, the Protestant countries of Europe never recognized the validity of the Papal grant. When the Spanish Ambassador complained to Elizabeth, in 1584, that Drake was infringing on Spanish rights under that grant, she refused to recognize the claim, haughtily answering, "that England knew nothing of a Papal gift, or any authority in the Pope to grant any land in world."

That great writer on National Law, Grotius, himself a Hollander, whose work, De Mare Juris, says Hallam, constituted an epoch in the affairs of Europe, denied that the Pope had any authority to grant the ocean to any power, because, in the nature of things, it was free to all. The same reasoning would apply, with equal force, to the unoccupied lands, of the then undiscovered world.

Spain, except in case of the Pacific Ocean, never made any such claim. Her position, in respect to the islands and continents of the new world, was like a mortgagee, who takes his mortgage to secure past and future advances. The Papal grant made it unnecessary for her to renew her application to the Pope on every fresh discovery.

Hence, in no point of view can this claim of the Dutch be maintained.

These are the grounds upon which the Dutch claimed the right to the ownership of any part of North America, and they are as untenable as

"The baseless fabric of a dream."

4. *Title by the de facto exercise of Dutch sovereignty over the Colony of New Netherland.*

To state the facts on this subject it will be necessary to commingle the acts of the Dutch and English as they concurrently transpired during the period in question.

In 1610 some Hollanders, still affected by the craze for a short route to China, fitted out some ships for a north passage thither, and on the 1st of February, 1611, the States-General perpetrated the most stupendous joke on record; they resolved to provide the adventurers with letters to the princes of the countries at which they might arrive, written in such language and characters as might be most useful ! These vessels, in the course of their explorations, landed at New York, and a commercial value in the furs obtained here led for the first time to a renewed voyage. In 1614 the owners of these ships, claiming and believing that they had discovered the harbor and bay of New York, petitioned the States General for an exclusive grant of trading to this territory, which was granted only to the extent of conferring upon them a monopoly among their own subjects. It was limited upon its face to this and was merely granted for the purpose of trade ; no territorial rights whatever, either by word or implication, were conferred. This monopoly was limited for three years, and subsequently renewed and extended to 1621.

The trade in furs proving profitable, they built three or four houses for the residence of those who remained, and a warehouse for the storage of their furs. One of their number was designated Governor of the colony, which had been continued from 1611.

While the Dutch were planting a fur trading colony on Manhattan Island, the French *emigres* were extending their colonies from Canada to Port Royal and Mount Desert for the pious purpose of converting the Indians.

When Sir Thomas Gates came to America in 1609, he brought with him to Jamestown, Virginia, or was followed by Capt. Thomas Argall, a regular old pirate, ready to pillage and destroy, to whom the Governor gave command. By virtue of his authority, and to supply the needs of the colony, in 1610, he visited the Penobscot region for cod and salmon. On his return he informed the Governor of the French settlements within the boundary of the Virginia grant, of which he had thus learned, and forthwith he equipped a fleet, and sailing to Maine drove the French from Port Royal and Mount Desert. Part of them he took prisoners and carried to Virginia, and the rest he inhumanly sent in an open boat to sea. Thus the Virginia colony asserted its

authority over the territory included in their grant,
and enforced the rights conferred upon them to
eject all trespassers. On his way back he stopped
in the port of New York and threatened the Dutch-
men there with extermination, such as he had
visited upon the French, if they did not recognize
the authority of Virginia. The defenseless Dutch-
men thereupon paid him the tribute which he had
demanded.

This statement has also been denied, but this destruction of the French settlements has been determined by the best possible authority, the report of
the Jesuits to Rome, and that being true, there is
inherent probability in the story of his treatment of
the Holland traders. Without citing the authorities,
it is sufficient to say that the Rev. Dr. De Dosta, a
thoroughly informed scholar on American history,
has established that the early Dutch settlers on
Manhattan island did, in 1613, acknowledge the
English sovereignty over the territory.

Again in 1619 or 1620, Captain Thomas Dormer,
an Englishman in the service of Sir Ferdinando
Gorges, touched at Manhattan on his way to New
England, and molested these Dutch settlers and
threatened to confiscate their property, whereupon
the Dutch promised "to come thether no moe."

The story of the exodus from England to Holland
and from Holland to America of those Godly men,
who are fondly remembered as the Pilgrim Fathers,
has been too often told to be repeated here. They
however bear a part in the legal history of New
York that must be mentioned. In 1617 they concluded to leave Holland, and they then determined
to settle in New York. Thereupon they sent a delegation to England to obtain a charter. Two years
elapsed before they were able to obtain a favorable
answer. Finally, in February, 1620, the first colony
of Virginia granted a patent to John Pierce and his
associates which entitled them to locate here, under
which they sailed in the *Mayflower*. Contrary to

their original intention, they landed on Plymouth Rock. Before debarking on the 11th day of November, 1620, in the cabin of the *Mayflower*, they designated themselves the loyal subjects of King James, who were undertaking to plant the first colony in the northern part of Virginia. In the meantime, the King had granted a separate charter to the second colony of Virginia, under the designation of the New England Colony, and on the first day of June, 1621, the President and Council of New England confirmed to the Pilgrims the Virginia charter by a patent which embraced New York.

On the 15th day of December, 1621, the English Privy Council addressed a letter to the British Minister at the Hague, demanding the removal of certain Hollanders who had, during the past year, intruded upon lands in that part of the north of Virginia called New England. Writing to the Lords of Council in February, 1621, the Ambassador says that he had made inquiry of merchants, the Prince of Orange and some of the States and learned that about four or five years since two particular companies of Amsterdam merchants began a trade in those parts betwixt 40 and 45, whither they had ever continued to send ships to fetch furs which was all their trade, for the providing of which they had certain factors resident there trading with the savages; but he could not learn of any colony either already planted there by these people or so much as intended. He would therefore demand of the Assembly to take information of the business of which they professed ignorance. Thereupon the British Ambassador presented a memorial and asserted in a letter accompanying it the incontestable right of the King of England to said country, both by original discovery and *jure primæ occupationis*, and that it was notorious to every one that he had by his letters patent granted quiet and full possession of the whole of said country to several private individuals.

It was this protest that secured the incorporation of the West India Company. For many years the patriot William Usselinx and his compatriots had besought the States-General to incorporate said company for the principal purpose of attacking the commerce of Spain. Into this company was merged the association of traders who had previously secured the Dutch monopoly of trading in the New Netherlands. The West India Company originally had no intention of colonizing in North America. It made New York a naval station, from whence its ships could intercept the golden argosies of Spain, in which it was so successful that within a few years it boasted that "it had exhausted the treasury of the King of Spain, by depriving him of so much silver which was as blood from one of the arteries of his heart." In return for this anticipated aid, the States-General incorporated a provision in the charter by which they obligated themselves to protect the Dutch territory in America.

"Hitherto," says Mrs. Booth, "the Dutch had looked on Manhattan only as a trading post. They did not think of making themselves homes in this new wild country, but dwelt in temporary huts, of the rudest construction, which scarcely protected them from the cold. But the English were exploring the coast and laying claim to all the country between Canada and Virginia, and the Dutch began to realize the importance of planting colonies in the new province, and thus securing their American possessions."

This charter was dated on the 3d of June, 1621, but the establishment of the company, although chartered, was postponed. The charter conferred · upon the corporators, for a period of twenty-one years, the exclusive right of trade in the Atlantic, from the tropic of Cancer to the Cape of Good Hope on the eastern, and from Newfoundland to the Straits of Magellan on the western shore. This was the extent of the West Indies. "Nothing could be more magnificent, nor more vague." The company was authorized to maintain fleets and armies, build forts and cities, carry on war, make contracts with the native princes, administer justice, appoint governors subject to the approval of the States-General to whom they were required to take oaths of allegiance. In return the company pledged itself to colonize the new territories (not any portion in particular), and to report its proceedings to the States-General. The government was vested in nineteen members, one appointed by the State, the others by five chambers of managers, established in the principal cities of Holland. Under this charter the Dutch had the same right to occupy Canada, Massachusetts, Florida and Brazil that they had to occupy New York.

About 1622 (most probably in 1620), although the only date given is 1622, certain Walloons and French who were desirous to go into Virginia, who were then residing in Holland, addressed the English Ambassador at the Hague, petitioning that his Majesty would permit fifty or sixty families as well Walloons as French, all of the reformed religion, to settle in Virginia a county under his obedience, that they might erect a town for their security, that they might have a grant of territory which they should hold from his majesty in such fealty as he might deem reasonable, under which conditions and privileges they would promise fealty and obedience such as faithful and obedient subjects owe their King and Sovereign Lord.

This petition was transmitted to Secretary Calvert, who acquainted his Majesty with it, by whom it was referred to the Virginia Company, to whom he had given all power by his letters patent to admit or exclude whom they pleased in that plantation, and thereupon the company were content to receive them upon certain conditions which were sent to the Hague to impart to the petitioners.

No further mention is made of this matter in the

State papers nor are the names of the petitioners mentioned. It adds to the weight of the argument that the Dutch people were fully advised of the English claim to the territory embraced in New York and that they asserted no right thereto. It affords color for an assertion that these were the identical people who actually founded the colony, for in 1623 the Amsterdam Chamber, to whose special care the province of New Netherland was consigned, despatched a vessel of large size with thirty families, mostly Walloons and French protestants, to found the colony. "These were, properly speaking, the earliest colonists of the province, the Dutch, who had previously emigrated thither, having been mere traders and temporary sojourners." In the same year the English prepared by force to attack the Hollanders in America, to give them fight and spoil and sink them down in the sea as they had previously served the French. But the Dutch entered into negotiation with England for a new treaty and the expedition never was despatched.

The English again asserted their rights here in January, 1624. On receiving information that there was a Dutch ship riding in the haven of Plymouth bound to a place in America which was comprehended in a grant made by his Majesty, an order was issued to the Vice-Admiral of Devon and the Mayor of Plymouth to make stay of the ship until otherwise ordered. It does not appear that it was ever permitted to prosecute the proposed voyage.

A treaty offensive and defensive against the unjust usurpations of Spain was solemnly made and concluded between the Lords States-General of the United Netherlands and his Majesty of England at Southampton, on the 7th day of Sept., 1625. This treaty gave to the respective parties the right of free ingress, egress and regress into all ports, havens, roads and creeks of the other with their men of war, merchant ships and prizes, and freedom of trade and commerce. In it there was nothing that could be tortured into any territorial concession.

In 1625 the jurisdiction of the first colony of Virginia over this territory was terminated by writ of *quo warranto*, which annulled the original Virginia charter. In May, 1626, Peter Minuit arrived at Manhattan as its Governor. His first act was the purchase of the Indian title. "Having thus become the lawful owners of the property," says Mrs. Booth, with more partiality for the Dutch than knowledge of the law, "the first care of the colonists was to provide for their personal safety. The English were constantly prowling about their coasts and threatening their destruction," to circumvent which Minuit, on the 9th of March, 1627, caused an amicable letter to be addressed Governor Bradford at Plymouth suggesting that they should maintain friendly relations. Of course it was intended to entrap the Governor into some admission of right, but Bradford was not so easily beguiled. He answered courteously, but suggested that the Dutch were trespassing on English territory. Alarmed by this answer Minuit replied a few weeks after vindicating the right of the States-General to the territory of New Netherland. Not content with this he communicated the matter to the Amsterdam Chamber, whereupon the West India Company petitioned the English government to accord to them the benefits of the treaty of Southampton. On the 5th day of September, 1627, this petition was granted by decree of the Privy Council, with this significant recital: "Whereas the companie of the West Indies in the united Provinces hath made humble suite unto his Maᵗⁱᵉ that their shipps employed thither either in trade or merchandize or on warfare for the weakening of the common enemy; might quietly pass on their intended voyages, both outward and homeward bound, without any molestation, stay or hindrance by his Maᵗⁱᵉˢ own shipps or those of his subjects employed with l^{rs} of marque to the southwards or elsewhere."

No clearer admission of English right could have been made than this petition. By the acceptance of the decree the Dutch were forever estopped from denying the right of England. It was the unqualified recognition of English sovereignty over that territory. Up to this time the Dutch had never asserted any title to New Netherlands. It was simply a trading company that had a monopoly as against other Hollanders of the furs and peltries of the province, and that had had there a local habitation and a name.

The benefits of the treaty of Southampton did not give the Dutch any title to the land, nor did the English so intend it. The original grant to the Virginia Company, the royal grants to the patentees of Connecticut, to Lord Sterling of Long Island and the lands adjacent thereto, and from the New England Company to the Plymouth Colony, all included New York. And every New England charter granted by Charles recited the original grant to the Second Colony of Virginia as embracing territory which included New York. Last of all the Governor-General of Ireland in 1632 granted to Sir John Plowden a patent to New York. On the principle that the last should be first, Plowden was the first to attempt to take possession of his property, he appeared and demanded of the Dutch that they should recognize his authority, which they refused to do upon the ground that his patent was invalid because the seal was broken, and as he had not a sufficient force at his command to compel submission to his claim, he found it expedient to retreat. But the English continuing thus to patent the land, continually asserted their right and title to the same.

Besides these royal grants the colonial Governors exercised jurisdiction over this territory. In 1628 the Governor of Virginia gave to Wm. Clayborne full power and authority to "saile into any the ryvers creekes portes and havens" within the degrees of 34 and 41 "and there to trade and truck with the Indians for furs skins corne or any other comodities of what nature or quality soever they bee."

The King of England also made similar grants.

In 1632 more vigorous measures were adopted to assert English sovereignty over New York. Captain Mason, interested in the New England patents, denounced the Dutch as interlopers "betwixt Cape Codd and Bay de la Warre in 40 degrees northerly latitude, being a part of that country which was granted to Sir Walter Rawleigh by Queene Elizabeth in Anno 1684 and afterwards to divers of her subjects under ye title of Virginia," and complained to the Government of their great trade. On the 19th of March, 1632, the Dutch vessel the *Eendracht* sailed from Manhattan Island for Holland loaded with furs and having as a passenger Governor Minuit, who had been recalled. By stress of weather it was forced into the port of Plymouth in England, and the vessel and cargo were seized by the British authorities upon the ground that the Dutch had invaded British rights in trading on English territory without a license. A diplomatic correspondence ensued, in which the English, as they invariably had done, claimed the territory by right of discovery and prior occupation. The Dutch West India Company laid claim to it because the New England and Virginia Colonies were chartered "upon the express condition that the respective incorporated parties should remain one hundred miles apart from each other, and have so much between them both." This statement, as the original charter shows, was incorrect, and if it were true would not countenance the Dutch claim. But it proves they knew the terms of the Virginia charter, and consequently they neither deceived others nor themselves by perverting its meaning. To this reason the Dutch ambassador added the further consideration that

they had acquired the title of the Indians. After
several months of negotiation the King of England
directed the release of the vessel with the express
reservation of his rights in the premises. The Company received the vessel without making any claim
for damages for its detention.

The next year there was the converse of this situation. In April, 1633, the *William*, a British vessel, British manned, came to New York, and in
spite of the Dutch protests ascended the Hudson to
trade with the Indians. The Dutch assembled in
force where the crew landed and drove them away.
The British Ambassador at the Hague thereupon
made a demand upon the Dutch West India Company for the damages thus sustained. The Company petitioned the States-General to interfere on
its behalf. After long consideration, on the 16th
day of October, 1634, the government declined to
interfere, and advised the Company to confer in this
matter with the English Ambassabor. Is this the
attribute of a sovereign? The Dutch were no pol-
troons. Invincible at sea, flushed with victory over
Spain, fearless of England, would they have thus
ignominiously refused to espouse the cause of their
own citizens, whose patriotic efforts had largely con-
duced to their success, if they were sovereign over
New Netherlands?

On the 7th of June, 1635, the president and council of New England surrendered its great charter to
the Crown for the purpose of having the land embraced therein divided into twelve provinces, which
the proprietors might enjoy in severalty. The
ninth of these extended from the Connecticut to
the Hudson, including Manhattan Island, and was
allotted to the Duke of Lenox.

In 1634 the Privy Council again ordered the detention of a ship of Holland lying at Cowes bound
for the Hudson River, and the prevention of any
others that might come thither for like purposes.

During the next fifteen years the troubles in England prevented much consideration of America. We can now with difficulty comprehend the situation as it then was. The whole country was called "the Wilderness," the horrors of which induced a criminal, to whom the choice was given of execution or transportation, to prefer hanging in England to living in America. Consequently the Dutch remained unmolested for the time being.

In 1643 William Kieft, who had become Governor of the little colony, planned and executed the most unjustifiable massacre of the Indians ever perpetrated in America under the delusion that he would awe the remainder into submission. In one week the country was desolated. On the fourth of March the panic-stricken Governor proclaimed a day of general fasting and prayer without atoning for his crime. The colony never recovered from the blow. The Indians destroyed the dwellings, the barns and the cattle of the settlers and prevented the cultivation of the soil. The distress had so increased that in the Fall they petitioned the Government to supply them with food to save them from starvation or with vessels to return them to Holland. The eight men, who were the chosen representatives of the colony, stated in one of the documents forwarded to the Government that the Indians had destroyed all the boweries or plantations upon the island beyond the fort, with the exception of only three, and that the inhabitants were in peril of their lives. The Government adopted a resolution that the population was neglected by the Company and in consequence decreasing.

In July, 1646, that doughty old Knickerbocker, Petrus Stuyvesant, was sent over to be the Governor of the province, and he found that while the Dutch had been suffering from the just resentment of the Indians, the English colonies had been prospering and flourishing and were rapidly approaching New York both from the east and the south. He therefore wrote to the States-General that unless the

colony was taken under the wing of the State instead
of being allowed to remain under a private corporation, the English would soon displace them.

In 1647 an agent of Lady Sterling, widow and
devisee of Lord Sterling, who held the Long Island
patent, demanded of Stuyvesant the surrender of
the territory.

In 1649 Stuyvesant negotiated with the Connecticut colony the settlement of the boundary line
between that colony and New Netherlands, but the
action of the colony was never ratified in England
and never became effectual. This was the nearest
approach ever made by the Dutch to any recognition
by England.

While the English colonies were rapidly increas-
ing in numbers and wealth, and were extending in
every direction, the affairs in New Netherland were
going from bad to worse, and in 1650 certain dele-
gates sent to Holland presented a petition to the
States-General in which they set forth the calamities
that had befallen them through the mismanagement
and neglect of the Dutch West India Company, by
which "their territory had become a desert and the
people impoverished, harassed, afflicted and reduced
to utter ruin, while New England was populous,
rich, prosperous and driving an immense trade and
commerce almost with the entire universe," and
recommended "in order to block the further prog-
ress of the English, that they should provisionally
set about hitching on to New Netherland the most
distant lands lying between the Dutch nation and
the English, which are yet vacant."

To add to their afflictions the British Parliament
in that year enacted that, after the 26th day of March,
1651, all vessels trading to Virginia and New England without English authority should be confiscated.
That the Dutch came within the purview and penal-
ties of this act was fully recognized by them in a
petition which the Dutch merchants addressed to
the States-General for relief. In the meantime, in

January, 1651, before the foregoing act was to take effect, England demanded that the Dutch should surrender some political refugees, which was refused. In the turmoil that ensued it was alleged that the English ambassador was insulted by the populace. Thereupon the Navigation Act was passed for the protection of English shipping against the Dutch, which resulted in war between the two countries.

In consequence of that, for the first time the States-General directly interfered in the affairs of the colony, and that only to this extent: On the 2d day of July, 1652, they directed Stuyvesant to take good care and be of a watchful eye respecting the persons he employed during the rupture between that State and England.

While this war was being waged, on the 2d day of February, 1653, on the anniversary of the feast of the Purification of the Virgin, commonly called Candlemas, the little colony on Manhattan Island became a city.

The following December, Cromwell became Lord Protector of England, and he immediately opened negotiations for peace, which was concluded in February, 1654. It was then that the States-General directed the Dutch West India Company to present to England their claim in the possible hope that it would meet with a favorable consideration, which has been before mentioned. Lord Thurloe, Cromwell's Prime Minister, asserted the justice of England's claim, both historically and legally, with convincing clearness and vigor.

In 1656 a census of the city was undertaken and its population was ascertained to be only one thousand, a large proportion of whom were negro slaves; so foreign to Dutch temperament and education was the effort at colonizing in America.

The encroachments of the English on the south induced Stuyvesant in 1659 to send a delegation to remonstrate with the authorities of Maryland in relation thereto, to which remonstrance the English

returned the answer they had invariably made that
they were the original owners and occupiers of all
the land known as Virginia and that they claimed
under the patent to Raleigh in 1584. Then it was
that the Dutch first claimed to derive their title
from the King of Spain and the Pope's donation.
They apparently abandoned the claim previously
made of title by purchase from the Indians, or discovery by Hudson.

The death of Cromwell, the downfall of his son
Richard and the restoration of Charles II. succeeded
one another with startling rapidity and changed
the aspect of affairs between England and Holland.
A revised and more obnoxious Navigation Act was
passed. In July, 1660, Lord Baltimore demanded
that the Dutch should surrender the land they occupied on Delaware Bay. Stuyvesant sent word to
Holland that the English were seeking to invade
the shores of the North River and to dispossess the
Dutch West India Company. All was gloom and
distress for these settlers.

In 1663 the English Royal Council for Foreign
Affairs, alleging that the Dutch had, of late years,
unjustly intruded upon and possessed themselves
of certain places on the main land of New England
and some islands adjacent, as in particular Manhatoes and Long Island, ordered a commission to
draw up a brief narrative of the Dutch invasion and
the means to make them acknowledge and submit
to his Majesty's government, or by force to compel
submission or expulsion. The direct result is unknown. Its purpose was apparent. The time had
arrived when England found it expedient and profitable to assert her claim. Lord Clarendon, Prime
Minister of Charles and father-in-law of James, the
Duke of York, was undoubtedly intriguing on behalf of his noble son-in-law to obtain this prize. In
furtherance of the scheme Clarendon purchased the
Sterling grant, and in the early part of 1664 Charles
sent royal commissioners, of whom Col. Nicholls was

one, ostensibly to visit the New England colonies with secret instructions hostile to the Dutch. On the 24th day of June, 1664, Charles granted to his brother James the famous royal charter to all lands from the Connecticut River to the Delaware Bay. James empowered Col. Nicholls to take possession. Stuyvesant obtained tidings of these proceedings which he sent to Holland, but they were treated as idle rumors unworthy of attention. An ancient friend and ally could not be guilty of such conduct. Meanwhile, a fleet was secretly sent to America, landing first at Boston and sailing thence to New York to enforce this claim. On the 2d day of September, 1664, the Dutch, unable to cope with the armed force England had sent, surrendered the colony and gave to the representative of the Duke of York peaceable possession, reserving to the inhabitants, in articles of capitulation, security in their person, inheritance, customs, conscience and religion.

This underhanded and cowardly act cost England dear. In consequence of it the Dutch declared war, and under Van Tromp, their great admiral, defeated the English, ascended the Thames and threatened to put London under contribution. The brave Dutch admiral had the audacity to fasten a new broom at his mast head to signify that he had made a clean sweep.

We are concerned with the legal aspect of this affair. If the Dutch were, as the English repeatedly asserted, interlopers and squatters, the law is very plain. It is the same with nations as matter of right as it is with individuals. If A occupies the land of B without right or title, and B ejects him by force or by fraud even, the manner and the time of the ejectment does not give A any redress as relates to ownership.

In 1665, the English having sued for peace, the treaty of Breda was made between England and Holland by New York, the cause of the war was conceded to England, and Surinam was surrendered to Holland to the great dissatisfaction of the English people, who valued the rich provinces of the East more highly than obscure and insignificant territory in the American wilderness.

England remained in quiet possession of New York until 1673, when the English and French declared war against Holland. In this emergency William of Orange was appointed Stadtholder, and he despatched the West India squadron, composed of twenty-seven vessels and sixteen hundred men, to attack the English. It destroyed the tobacco fleet of Virginia, and on the 28th day of July, 1673, sailed into the port of New York and demanded its surrender. The English, unable to resist with this formidable array, yielded on the following day. On the 8th of August the admirals of the fleet placed Sir Anthony Colve in command of the Province, and the Dutch became, by conquest, the lawful sovereigns of New York. The conquest, however, availed the Dutch very little. The Prince of Orange, with true statesmanship, determined to concentrate all his resources against the King of France, and therefore restored New Netherland to England. On the 8th of February, 1674, the treaty of Westminister transferred the title to the King of Great Britain.

Upon this the question arose whether the patent to the Duke of York revived by virtue of the acquisition of the territory by the English. The crown lawyers, to whom it was submitted, unanimously held that it did not. The grant had been extinguished by the Dutch conquest, and now belonged to the crown by the English conquest.

Thereupon Charles, on the 29th day of June, 1674, executed to James a new patent in the identical words (except its date), but without any reference whatever to the first patent. Many well informed persons have fallen into the error of supposing that this was a confirmatory grant, but James had no title whatever to confirm and the error has arisen from a failure to appreciate the exact situation.

The effect of these grants has been adjudicated upon by the Supreme Court of the United States in Martin *vs.* Waddell, 16 Peters, 369, which involved the title to lands in New Jersey embraced therein. It was held that the right of the King to make these grants was unquestionable; that they were made to enable the Duke of York to establish a colony to be governed according to the laws and usages of England; that they created a viceroyalty; and the people were subjects of Great Britain. It has also been held by the same tribunal that the making of the grants heretofore mentioned from the days of Henry VII. to James was the continual declaration of the Crown of its sovereignty over the lands so patented. James's representative granted to the City of New York all the waste and unpatented lands. And in the changes from the Dutch to the English and from the English to the Dutch the only reservation made was that which accorded with international law, that the rights of private ownership and all succession under wills should be respected, and the Dutch claimants obtained from the English authorities confirmations of their previous grants. Once more the political title, that is the title to all unpatented lands, reverted to the Crown when James on the death of Charles succeeded to the throne of England.

In this brief summary of the events that transpired here it will be seen that under the law of nations as it has always been declared in both Europe and America the English were the lawful owners by right of discovery under governmental authority, perfected by taking possession long before the Dutch ever landed here, and continued by assertion of such ownership down to the time of the conquest.

On the other hand the Dutch were interlopers, intruders, squatters. They had no title in fee to the land before 1673. A squatter's title may become valid by lapse of time, but there is no statute of limitations against nations. When national or political usurpation ceases it is obliterated. This has been so decided in regard to the so-called Confederate States government. When it ended it was as if it had never existed. Its ordinances and decrees afforded no justification and gave no color of right to any acts done thereunder. Prior to 1673 the law of England was the only law that can now be recognized as the law of the land. Whatever may be the effect of the Dutch-Roman law upon roads and highways, respecting which there is a wide difference of opinion, in places where Holland has had jurisdiction, it is immaterial in this case. That law never prevailed in this colony except for the few months that elapsed between the end of July, 1673, and the beginning of February, 1674.

4. *The objections made to this claim answered.*

One might be curious to know what answers have been made to these views, and therefore we state all that has heretofore been presented as the result of the laborious research of the counsel for the Elevated Railroad in New York who are interested in maintaining the proposition that certain roads in New York were of Dutch origin and governed by their law. This is what they say :

"The *de facto* exercise of sovereignty over the colony of New Netherland by the States General of Holland is shown : (1.) By the recognition of their sovereignty in petitions and other papers emanating from the inhabitants of New Netherland. (2.) By acts and resolutions of the States-General pertaining to New Netherland. (3.) By expressions employed by the magistrates of New Netherland in patents for land and other official papers. (4.) By the recognition of their sovereignty in diplomatic intercourse between the States-General and the foreign powers in relation to matters other than treaties. (5.) By the exercise of judicial authority by the States-General in matters arising in New Netherland. (6.) By the recognition of the previous authority of Holland by the English, after the surrender in 1664 and again in 1674."

We have quoted their language word for word in full, and on it judgment might be asked in favor of the English claim. For conceding that every one of the six propositions could be proved as fully as might be presumed from the statement there is nothing whatever that in the slightest degree invalidates the preceding argument which leads inevitably to the determination that England by right of discovery and possession became and never ceased to be the sovereign of New York.

But such argument is deserving of respectful and detailed consideration and the more it is considered the weaker will the Dutch case appear.

(1). In 1643 the eight men who have been heretofore mentioned subscribed their petition "your High Mightinesses' faithful servants and subjects." The petition of the Commonalty in 1649 was addressed to the States-General "our Most Excellent Sovereigns," and its appendix to "our Most Serene Sovereigns." The address of the colonists determines nothing. Agency and tenancy are not established by the declarations of the agents and tenants to bind third parties. For the question is not what they called themselves but what they were.

(2). Under the second head they cite orders of the Dutch Government in the affairs of the Dutch West India Company and in the affairs of individuals. No one disputes that the Dutch West India Company was incorporated by the States-General, and consequently the government had control over its affairs. Does legislation over the affairs of the

New York Central Road make its tenants citizens
of the State of New York ? Does the appointment
of government directors in the Union Pacific Railroad make it a national road ? If the law of New
York required the appointment of the president of
the elevated road by the State, and that he should
swear allegiance thereto, would that make the road
over which he presided the property of the State
and its servants State officers ? Besides these, there
were two instances in which the State interfered in
private affairs, first in 1641 and again in 1652, author-
izing particular individuals to devise property in
New Netherland. Hollanders in their native land
and in its colonies where they owned the soil must
have had by general law power to devise, and this
express request and grant must have been a recognition that no such power existed here These two
cases were covered by the terms of one of the articles
of capitulation in 1554, of which we shall speak hereafter.

(3). Under the third claim there are four principal subdivisions—purchased from Indians, grants
by the Company, Stuyvesant's title, and declarations
in 1673—from the conquest to the surrender. The
Indian grant recitals were substantially as follows :
" We the Director and Council of New Netherland
on the Island of Manhattan in Fort Amsterdam,
under the jurisdiction of their High Mightinesses'
the Lords, the States-General of the United Netherlands and the General Incorporated West India
Company do by these presents: publish and
declare, that on this day, the date under
written before us, in their proper persons
came and appeared, &c." The utmost that such
grants could convey, as has been decided by the Supreme Court, is a usufructuary use (void in this case);
but waiving that question, it nowhere appears that
the States-General or the Company ever knew of
his assumption on the part of the Governor who

L. of C.

had no authority to use the State's name. The same is true in the title used by the Governor in his colonial court and in the private grants. There nowhere appears either the slightest authority, knowledge or recognition for, or of, the bombastic rhetoric of the conceited Governor who was only a servant of the Company and had no right to use the name of the State. The last stand on a different footing. The conquerors had the right to speak in the name of the States-General then, and from thenceforth until the end of their occupation; but that did not affect the past and gave them no authority to make any declarations of the past; it was no part of the *res gestæ*, as the courts would say.

(4). Under this heading two instances, the William and the Eendragt, are given as showing English recognition of Dutch sovereignty. In the first the Dutch Ambassador wrote to his Government that complaint had been made to him about the exclusion of the English from the Hudson, thus recognizing the control and authority actually possessed by the States-General in New Netherland is the inference drawn therefrom. In other words if an American citizen were driven from the coast of Spain by an English ship and should make complaint and the British minister should write to his own government that complaint had been made to him about the matter, that would be American recognition of England's authority in Spain. Not by any means. It recognized that the trespassers were subjects of the power from which they demanded compensation. So the admission that the Dutch were in possession without right, was a declaration that they were trespassers and intruders who were to be removed by the States-General.

(5). The Dutch undoubtedly did exercise judicial authority in New Netherland in cases of a personal character—as are all cited—and perhaps also relating to realty; so did the Confederate States, in the time of their usurpation ; so has been done everywhere by organized mobs and rebels ; so it is among the banditti ; but when the force that sustains such exercise of authority disappears the judicial authority vanishes.

(6). The confirmatory grants did recognize that previous grants had been made and for a good consideration confirmed them. Parallel instances frequently occur in real estate titles at the present day. A buys of B land which in fact C owns. He then purchases of C the real title and takes a deed confirming his title and possession. No one for an instant would dream of asserting that C thereby recognized that B was the true owner.

These are the facts, a beggarly array, on which those who have a personal professional interest in upholding the Dutch title rely.

In opposition to all the acts of the Dutch from which title might be presumed, one omission is very significant. When Cabot first landed he took possession of the continent in the presence of witnesses on behalf of the English sovereign; so did Ralegh's colonists at Roanoke; so did Columbus on behalf of Ferdinand and Isabella; so did De Soto and all the great discoverers. This became so universal that Lord Stowell in The Fama, 5 Robt. Adm. R., said : "Even in newly discovered countries where a title is meant to be established for the first time, some act of possession is usually done and proclaimed as a notification of the fact." This the Dutch never did in New York. This was not omitted through ignorance. For when they subsequently took possession of the land on the South River, as they called the Delaware, they placed upon a pole a piece of tin stamped with the Holland arms to signify its sovereignty there.

There is also a little law of which they make much, but which is without authority.

Judge Murray Hoffman wrote a treatise on the Estates and Rights of the Corporation, a self-imposed task, which however valuable in its information had not the least claim to authority. In it he says: "It cannot be questioned at this day that the *right* of discovery and occupation of New Netherland, and particularly of Manhattan Island, was in the Dutch, and that the claims of the English were unfounded." And more of the like dogmatic and unsupported assertion. And this he says with full knowledge of Chief-Justices Marshall and Taney's opinions.

Oftentimes a bold and unblushing falsehood deceives the very elect. It was so in this respect. There came before the Court of Appeals the case of Dunham *vs.* Williams, 37 N. Y., 251, involving a Dutch title at Flatbush. The arguments of the counsel engaged were considered by the reporter to be too insignificant to be reported. Judge John K. Porter wrote an opinion which inferentially said that the Dutch did have title here before the capitulation, citing therefor three authorities, one from Louisiana, which might expound the civil law, but not the Dutch rights here; another argument of Charles O'Conor, which quoted Hoffman, and then Hoffman. So when it came to the crucial test it is Hoffman unadulterated and unsupported. Turning to Mr. O'Conor's argument he will be found to have expressed himself thus guardedly: "This colony was first settled by Holland and was consequently governed *de facto* at the time of its settlement by the civil law." The italics are his. He subsequently denied that the Dutch ever had a title here.

In the case of the Canal Company *vs.* The People, 5 Wend., 445, Chancellor Walworth says: "It is a matter of history that this province was always claimed by the English by right of discovery and not as a conquered country, and that no part of the civil law as such, except that which was derived from England, has ever been in force in this colony. The province was granted to the Duke of York as part of the domain of the crown, several months before the surrender to Sir Richard Nicholls and before any attempt had been made to take possession by force. The guaranty to the Dutch settlers of the peaceable enjoyment of their possessions did not alter the nature of the British claim to the country. It was a just and wise policy on the part of the Duke's Government; by it he retained in the colony a great number of industrious, intelligent and valuable inhabitants, of whom and their descendants even at this day the State has much reason to be proud. After a short struggle they submitted peaceably to the Duke's claim, and subsequently they obtained patents from the crown for the lands they originally held. The territory being thus claimed and established as a British colony, the common law of England became the fundamental law of the province."

In Canal App. vs. People, 17 Wend., 609, the Court says of a patent there under consideration: "The original Dutch grant being made, the civil law which prevailed in Holland, and which if brought to this State by the Dutch," &c. Mark the if !

In Mayor vs. Hart, 95 N. Y., 450, Finch, J., uses this language in relation to a grant made in 1666, two years after the grant to the Duke of York: "We must assume such to have been the common law at the date of the grant. Two years earlier the Dutch had surrendered Amsterdam to Col. Nicholls, who with an armed force asserted the right and authority of the Duke of York and the English Government. The common law of England entered the city with him." That assertion was sufficient for the case before the Court, and cannot be construed as deciding that it was not here before, for that question was not before the Court.

Gould vs. Hudson River R.R., 6 N. Y., 522;

People *vs.* Canal Company, 33 N. Y., 461, and People *vs.* Ferry Co., 68 N. Y., 71, have no reference to the Dutch. They involve only the common law right of navigable waters.

In U. S. *vs.* Perot, 98 U. S. (80th), 428, and in Freemont *vs.* U. S., 17 How., 542, the judicial notice which the Court is bound to take of the antecedent law was Spanish, a legal, regular and recognized authority, not the law of a usurper. Would the Supreme Court take judicial notice of Confederate laws?

Some stress has also been laid upon certain remarks of England's greatest jurist, Lord Mansfield, in the celebrated case of Campbell *vs.* Hall (1 Cowp., 211; 20 State Trials, 239), as militating against the English claim.

That case was so complicated and important that it was elaborately argued four times before a decision was rendered. It involved the validity of a tax imposed upon exports from the island of Granada, imposed by the King of England after it had been taken by the British arms in open warfare from the French King. Cases of conquest, including the conquest of New York from the Dutch, were instanced by Lord Mansfield as showing historically the right of the conqueror to lay down the law for the vanquished, and the nature and extent of that right. This was his language:

" After the conquest of New York, in which most of the Dutch remained, King Charles II. changed the form of their constitution and political government by granting it to the Duke of York, to hold of his crown under all the regulations contained in the Letters Patent. No question was ever started before, but that the King has a right to a legislative authority over a conquered country."

The error that has been made is in applying this first sentence quoted to the first grant to James in 1664. The error is manifest when it is observed that he is speaking of conquest and a conquered country as applied to open warfare between the French and English. The grant in 1664 was made in a season of profound peace not after conquest, but in 1674, after a brief but bloody struggle in which the English had sustained a series of humiliating defeats and had been compelled to sue for peace, and therefore the illustration was opposite to the case under consideration.

Another line of argument has been adopted by Mr. Richard Webster, who says in an opinion in the Lauderdale Peerage Case :

" Very inconvenient legal consequences may flow from a successful maintenance, in the United States at least, of the contention that English dominion and sovereignty over Manhattan Island and the Province of New York and all the lands therein were valid and complete in 1609, when Henry Hudson arrived, and continued valid and complete down to 1664, and that the Dutch during all that period were mere intruders. For if English dominion, sovereignty and title were thus valid and complete, then by the accepted rules of public law, both English and American, the aboriginal Indians had from 1609 to 1664 no right, without English permission, to convey any portion of their lands to Holland, its officers, subjects or citizens, and therefore all titles to lands depending solely on such grants or conveyances were and are null and void."

Inconvenient legal results cannot determine the administration of law, and none can flow from the successful maintenance of English sovereignty over this territory on account of making Indian titles null and void, for there are no such titles, the law of nations having always been that the Indians had none to convey. His protest, however, involves the concession for which we have contended, that the Dutch obtained nothing from the Indians if the English had any rights whatever.

No Judge has made a more prolonged or thorough

study of the early history of New York than Judge
Truax. The question of the Dutch title has been before him thrice in his judicial capacity. As a de-
scendant of the issue of the first marriage ever celebrated in the colony his personal prejudices or pre-
delictions could not have been hostile to the Dutch.
In Mortimer *vs.* N. Y. El. R.R., 6 N.Y. Supplement,
898, he presents an admirable condensed statement of
the situation, and concludes : "I am of the opinion
that the fee of the Bowery and of the other streets
in the City of New York that are known as Dutch
Streets never was in the Dutch government ; and
that it was prior to the Revolution bound by the
rules of the common law and not by the rules of the
Dutch civil law. While the Dutch were in actual
possession this execution of the common law was
suspended, just as during the late Rebellion the
execution of the laws of the United States could not
be enforced in some of the Southern States."

In a concurring opinion Judge Freedman says in
reference to the authorities cited by Judge Truax :
"These decisions proceeded upon the theory that the
claim of the Dutch was contested by the English
from the very start, not because they questioned the
title given by discovery, but because they insisted
on being themselves the rightful claimants under
that title, and that the claim of the English was finally decided in their favor by the sword. That being so, it follows that in contemplation of present law,
neither the Dutch nor the Roman law ever prevailed
in the State of New York *de jure* and that the common law of England must be deemed to be the common source of all our law."

In the equity case of Hine *vs.* El. R.R. depending
in the Superior Court recently decided, Judge Truax
amplifies the history he gave in the Mortimer decision by citations from Ogelby's America, the Historical Society Publications, Hakluyt and Kohl's
History of Maine, all of which are in confirmation
of what he had previously written.

The opinions delivered by Judge Truax in the first two cases above cited were so convincing that the General Term of the Supreme Court in the law case of Hine *vs.* El. R.R. depending in that Court, unanimously reversed a judgment dismissing the complaint pronounced by Van Brunt, P. J., who held that the Dutch Roman law prevailed here. This reversal was based upon those decisions.

So the weight of authority is on the English side. These decisions have been made after a full discussion of all the earlier decisions and with an exhaustive review of the historical facts. For, however weighty the opinion of the Courts may be in disposing of questions of law, they cannot bind in historical or scientific matters. They adjudicate upon the facts as they are known and are as liable to error as the Court of the Inquisition in the trial of Gallileo.

What is the practical result of this discussion?

The counsel for the Elevated Railroad, if we understand him correctly, answers that it is nothing that he is willing to concede all for which we contend ; it is true that under the common law the rights of property owners adjoining highways extends to the centre, but under the Dutch law they are limited to the side, and as the grant was made by the Dutch authorities it must be construed according to Dutch law and the English confirmative deed ratified only what had been previously obtained.

In other words, although we admit that the Dutch were squatters and had no rights *de jure* you must treat them as rightful sovereigns. For if they were the legal owners no more could be claimed.

An exact statement carries its own refutation.

This must be the law governing such a case ; the common law of England always prevailed here although not always recognized. The Dutch governor was a private individual, granting property on English soil, and consequently the grant extended to the centre of the highway under English law ; just as if the man had been in England.

What force then do you give to the *de facto* government? Do you not ignore it altogether in such a construction? Not entirely—when the English resumed their rightful authority, yes: while the Dutch held possession, no. They could then use the highway as if they were its rightful owners; this and nothing more.

The language of Mr. O'Conor in Wetmore *vs.* Story, 22 Barb., 440, "that when Britain expelled the intrusive power of Holland and resumed her lawful possession, she adopted the existing settlement, with its existing customs," is cited against this proposition, and if the adoption were as broad as Mr. O'Conor states it, and the word "customs" could be construed to mean all the Dutch laws, there might be some force in it. But it is not necessary to construe the word, for it has its own limitation, and the law of eminent domain is thereby excluded. This was the provision in the Articles of Capitulation in 1664:

"XI. The Dutch here shall enjoy their own customs concerning their inheritances."

It is not necessary to discuss the distinctions between the *viæ publicæ* and the *viæ vicinales*, the highways and byways or country roads, and nothing could be added to the brief of Mr. Van Nest on that subject. Nor is it necessary to pursue the line of argument so ably presented to the Court by Mr. Cowles.

It is conceded that the historical question which the Court takes judicial notice of, Hunter *vs.* N. Y. C. & W. R.R., 116 N. Y., 615, underlies and determines the whole matter if the Court of Appeals entertains the views herein expressed, and as to that there can be no reasonable doubt.

The City of New York has had the most romantic legal history of any place on earth. Its title was acquired by England by original discovery; the grant to Cabot reverted to the Crown by his death; the grant to Raleigh escheated on judgment in attainder; the grant to Virginia was cancelled by *quo warranto* proceedings; the grant to New England was voluntarily surrendered; the title of the Dutch in 1673 was acquired by conquest in 1674; and the grant to James passed to the Crown on his accession to the throne. There was one other possible transmission which did not take place, England never bought it. Hers by original right, hers it continued to be until 1673, and her laws governed it (except for a few months in 1673 and 1674), until it was wrested from her by successful Revolution in 1776, when the United States became a nation.

www.ingramcontent.com/pod-product-compliance
Lightning Source LLC
Chambersburg PA
CBHW031804090426
42739CB00008B/1155